A Hand to Hold

D1565807

Also by Tony Howarth

Wild Man of the Mountain

A Hand
to Hold

Three dramas in verse by
Tony Howarth

Broadstone

Library of Congress Control No. 2022940881

ISBN 978-1-956782-15-8

Design by Larry W. Moore
&
Stephanie Potter

Broadstone Books
An Imprint of
Broadstone Media LLC
418 Ann Street
Frankfort, KY 40601-1929
BroadstoneBooks.com

CONTENTS

OUT FROM THE MONSTER'S CLAWS

John Smith arrived in Virginia on the *Susan Constant*
in 1607. While official history trumpets him
as a hero, a man of courage, vision, and persistence
who carved a gem of national pride out of the merciless
wilderness, it also admits he was an autocratic,
narcissistic, self-aggrandizing brute who succeeded
only by bullying, demanding total loyalty, imposing
a cruel discipline.

He that will not worke shall not eate.

The history books also tell of a teenage girl,
Anne Burras, who arrived in October 1608
on a supply ship, *The Mary and Margaret,*
who then married a laborer, John Laydon,
later giving birth to four daughters.

But a television documentary detailed an archeological dig
which unearthed, in what was a kitchen midden,
the skull of a 14-year old girl scarred with knife scratches
which suggested cannibalism.

Folklore has yet another story to tell, whispered
by a tour guide at the James Towne reconstruction,
a tale that made me tremble to imagine
how dehumanizing it can be to struggle
for survival in a landscape presided over
by someone like John Smith.

Something I've not done
is following me
I haven't done it again and again
so it has footsteps
like a drumstick that's grown old and never been used

—W. S. Merwin

I am waiting

         anyone defying John Smith
                        watch out
            he'll narrow his eyes
         a flash of flame inside

I want to slug him in that face of his
           dump him in the river
      shove his head under   choke him

                    the bugger

she's what   fourteen   fifteen

      he straps her into the stocks
                    feeds her
       to his revved-up mob

~

waiting
Ould Drasty
                    minute I arrived that's what they called me
            put me in my place
                            bottom of the nobody list
        Bugger wanted me sent back right away
                    gray hair and droopy shoulders

            out of his line of sight
                                    put me in the saw pit
            underneath the logs we shape into battlements
        breathing sawdust all day long

                                        bastard
                his mob   like barking dogs
                                ragging a squirrel

unforgivable
                she with her hands locked in the boards
                    they shower kitchen waste on her
            bones that lodge in her hair
        their fingers skritch beneath her skirt
                            badger her breasts

            nothing she can do but shriek
        and weep
so I am nobody
                    Ould Drasty
        a nobody
                waiting

                to help her   somehow
                        he'll tear me to shreds   I know

even so   I must

∾

night
      the moon beaming down on us

                                men gone to their cots
                        sentry lost in the shadows
        I slash my axe against the ropes

                three times
                    four
                        they snap
I pry the stocks open   hold her hand
                                  she howls
                I flatten my arm across her mouth
        she bites   kicks me away
            foots it like a frantic rabbit

                          into the forest
   my twisted foot
        I stumble behind

∼

she plunges through the grasping undergrowth
                squashing it
        splintered branches
                        left dangling

                I reach out my hand to stop her
            don't you she yells
                    whacks   and whacks me

        face to face
                she scoops a handful of dirt
                            chucks it bang in my eyes
    not to look at me like that
                    like all the others

                    I tell her   no   I'm looking
            at someone young in dreadful danger

rush on your feet into the shrubbery
        leave a give-away path
                            they'll track you down
            haul you back

    she screams at me
never!   not going back!   no!
                    never!

    poaching on blueblood estates back home
I've learned how to survive in the woods
        footprints soft and silent
lift the branches   lift the feet

    walk in the dark of night
sleep during the day

                                        another danger
                        Powhatan hunters in the forest
                 got knives and arrows   out for blood
                perhaps James Towne is safer
        she pummels my chest
spit flying   *NEVER!!   NEVER!!*

    says she wants to meet the Powhatans
ask them to take her to one of their own

                    Namontack
     they spent time together on the Mary Margaret
he smiled at her   talked to her   in English

    who knows why he was taken to London
why he was tied to the mast on the way back

    she says everyone snubbed her
but he laughed   chatted with her

    she shared the food she was given
brought him a blanket

    ∼

as we walk
       in the silence of darkness
       stranger to this wilderness
       I hear a familiar voice
       an owl   hooting
       as if I'm walking
       in the woods back home
       mournful   sad
       by ourselves
       in the endless forest

～

I don't know what I'm doing
wasn't it right?
wasn't it?
what I did?
took her away
from Bugger's claws

~

I hear the singing of a brook
should I maybe   suggest we follow it?

keep the water by our side so if we stray
we'll shut away confusion
always a place to come back to?

≈

we find a spot to settle in daylight
hack branches and shrubs

with the axe I carry in my satchel
build a leaning shelter

watch her wriggle inside
give her my coat to wrap herself

stretch myself out on a bed of weeds
hidden beneath a blanket of branches

~

her sobbing wakes me
I want her silent

I beg her to be calm   John Smith
for certain has soldiers out looking

with the brook singing past
she weeps me her helpless
                    what could have been

six of them   five sisters and a brother
often clustered in front of the fire

loved to sit warm and weave cat's cradles
loved the songs their mother taught them

for all the day long   owl sits in a tree
and when the night comes   away flies she

when their mother died sudden in her bed
the sisters were bargained off by their father

scullery maids   farmhouse helpers
brother ran away   not to be seen again

she shares her story
and I'm here to listen
don't know what to think
unaccustomed
people don't tell me
their stories

she's calm at last . I give her a twinkle of bread
stashed in my satchel for hungry moments

watch her crumple it   stuff it in her mouth
tell her how my body has been battered for years

maybe fifty   could be more
I do it ever by hiding invisible

as with Bugger Smith out looking for us
we hide by night   sleep by day

something I've not ever done
daring to share
                        nose, nose, jolly red nose
                        and who gave you that jolly red nose
            so sotted drunk
            I passed out sleeping on the street
          . a ship's crew carousing past
            for a lark they pick me up
            dump me on board
            wake me next morning
            surrounded by ocean

            for a moment   Ould Drasty
            I have her smiling

~

she scrambles back inside her shelter
I'm left wishing I had a fire to my feet

staring into the flames and pondering

how she astonishes

when we walk I feel her on my heels
begging me to pick up speed
desperate to escape her blistering memories

as when

the *Mary Margaret*
pulled into the dock
with her
on the deck
for all to see

stood beside
the man and wife
she was bargained to

because a child
born in James Towne
will bring him fame
in London
Bugger Smith
thinks only of himself
staggered her away
to raffle her
as a wife

the blacksmith won
rushed her to the church

asked Priest
to bless their union

lugged her
to his smithy
threw her
on the ground
to have her

everyone listening
and sipping spit
he snarling
she shrieking

but the child

fought him off

wriggled free

left him fuming

Priest in a sermon
condemned her

tis sacred duty
a wife must
bear a child

Priest and Bugger
godly righteous
strapped her
into the stocks

more Jesus
than they will ever be

∼

I hate Priest
worse than I hate Bugger

remember how
in a church at home
I sheltered for the night
hidden in the undercroft
and the cleaners came to clean
smashed all the stain glass windows
toppled the statues
everything but a small crucifix
hanging on the wall
I took Him for myself
talked to Him
like I'm talking now

but Priest caught me
stomped on Him
like putting out a fire
my companion
my treasure
called me heathen
sat me in the stocks
for praying to an idol

~

as we walk

half the night gone   under a full moon
we come to where the brook spills over a ledge

gurgles into a pond   a place for the water
to rest on its way to the river and sea

the bushes all around look like blackberry
we pick and choke down handfuls

tumble flat along the edge of the pool
drink   laughing   drench our faces

far enough away from Bugger Towne
I feel safe settling in the open

sleep with nothing above our heads but sky
then   during the night   I hear

rocks rattling   splashing noises
see her sitting in the pool

washing her hair

~

next morning

      gone

          I wipe my tears

     take the risk and call out for her

                  hello-o-o

I've never before walked a path
         with someone else

         is she following the brook

      I can only hope

         she'll not return to Bugger Towne

       if straight into the endless forest
    she'll be lost
         one tree like every other

                 hello-o-o

    she knows what she wants
          no matter what
              gone   to find it

   I'll wait here
      if she finds him Namontack
         if the Powhatans are kind to her
     if he welcomes her
         but if not
   she'll remember the pond
      the brook will guide her
  where I'll be waiting

if I go back to Bugger Towne
he'll hang me
waiting
by our pond
our waterfall
our brook
its song well sung
so comforting

first   Ould Drasty   make a shelter
plenty of branches for wattles
plenty of mud   from the pool
to daub between them
a place for when it rains
for when it turns cold

for her to come back to

NOTES

Drasty is a Middle English word meaning "useless."

The fragments of song:

> *for all the day long   owl sits in a tree*
> *and when the night comes   away flies she*

and

> *nose, nose, jolly red nose*
> *and who gave you that jolly red nose*

are taken from a folksong of the period, *Jolly Red Nose*,
found in *Folksongs of Old English*,
by Maddy Prior and Tim Hart

BESIDE THE RED DEAF WALL

Outside a prison in Leningrad, at the height of Stalin's
Terror, crowds, mostly women, the poet Anna Akhmatova
among them, waited in line to deliver food, messages,
gifts for the inmates.

One woman whispered to her, asking her if she could
describe what they were going through. Akhmatova's
answer was a simple "Yes."

But my imagination insisted there was more to the
conversation. I pictured her comforting the woman
at the wall. I listened to the passions woven into her
poetry, translated fragments from the Russian
and began to write, the words of her poetry embraced
by quotation marks

у меня сегодня много дела
надо память до конца убить
надо чтоб душа окаменела
надо снова научиться жить

—*Anna Akhmatova*

I have today a lot to do
I need to kill my memory
I need to petrify my soul
I need again to learn how to live

EKATARENA
we're outside a prison in Leningrad
at the height of the tyrant Stalin's Terror
we come to this prison every day
to wait in line in front of the wall
with food   messages   gifts
shove them through a tiny window
to an officer with a piggy grunt

do we get to see our husbands   sons
boyfriends   fathers?

CHORUS
No

EKATARENA
are we certain
          they get our gifts and messages?

CHORUS
No

EKATARENA
but we live with hope
our voice of hope
our poet Anna Akhmatova
if she publishes her poetry
Stalin threatens all sorts of punishments
so she doesn't publish
but she writes
what's in her heart she writes
we whisper her words to one another
memorize them   keep them to ourselves

          ANNA
          "I have today a lot to do"

          EKATARENA
          "I need to kill my memory"

ANNA & EKATARENA
"I need to petrify my soul"

ALL
"I need again to learn how to live"

EKATARENA
someone new has come to join us
stands   looking lost
we turn away
we don't want her to see our faces
don't know if we can trust her

ANNA
but she's weeping

CHORUS
"Tears for the pain that burns her heart."

EKATARENA
and she carries a coat
a shoulder bag
stands in the street
pleads for help

OLGA
a knock on the door
        my brother pushed
    me into the
                closet hid me behind
    the coats and jackets
                    I heard thumps
        voices
    violent

ANNA
and then—

EKATARENA
        silence

OLGA
all I could find out—
he's behind that wall

            CHORUS
            "The prison's massive iron gates
            Shut and tightly locked against us"

        •

OLGA
I can't do it
        I can't
    standing here
makes it real
            join you
    for what
for what
    standing here
            as if it's a funeral
I caaaaaan't

EKATARENA
one long shriek   agony
and she breaks away
Anna chases her
grabs her by the shoulder bag

            CHORUS
            "The mountains bend before the grief.
            The river waters flow no longer."

EKATARENA
she collapses
her knees crack on the floor
I watch Anna jump
to kneel beside her

reach out but she pushes Anna away
slaps her
and Anna doesn't even wince

ANNA
I don't want you helping them
allowing them to win

OLGA
I'm here to go
    go to that stinking window
  and give them this coat
    when they knocked on the door he
was in his shirtsleeves

EKATARENA
she throws the coat into the street
stands   frantic
tugs a loaf of bread out of her bag
breaks it in half
shrieks at it   shatters one half of it
scatters the crumbs in Anna's face
I reach out to stop her
but she runs like a rabbit
turns to face us   crouches
fists folded for a fight

OLGA
this bread
    this bread
  because knowing
      them they'll never feed him
        so why did I bring it
  this fucking bread

CHORUS
"As if she's rudely beaten back.
On her feet alone she staggers."

ANNA
you're not alone you know

OLGA
oh come on
        not alone because you're
                crowding together in line
        shuffling forward an inch at a time?

ANNA
we hold each other's hands
stand in quiet defiance

OLGA
how does that help my brother
                what has he done
he drives a tram
        all day he drives his tram
staring at the tracks in the street
        they tell me nothing
nothing except where he is
        just nod and glare what
would a tram driver do
that they should grab him away

EKATARENA
calm

OLGA
        how do I   I don't
I don't know
is he even in there
                        is he still alive

ANNA
calm

OLGA
calm
what does calm do for me
   how does calm bring him back to me

EKATARENA
Anna wraps both arms around her
holds her tight
speaks in soothing softness

          ANNA
           "I pray not only for myself
           But for everyone who's standing here
           In the biting cold, in the summer heat,
           Beside the red deaf wall."

EKATARENA
they stay locked together
til slowly they pull apart

OLGA
who are you?

ANNA
a woman who stood behind you in the line

OLGA
so?

ANNA
who are you?

OLGA
no need for you to know

ANNA
I'd like to

OLGA
I'd like you not to

       ANNA
       "The muse, my sister, stared in my face."

       CHORUS
       "Her gaze burning crystal bright."

EKATARENA
which makes her a poet

OLGA
a poet!   oh my
living the wild life
a man on each arm
serenading the moon
smelling the roses
the gentle breeze floating from the river
never looking at the agony around us

ANNA
I stood   in line
               looking at *you*

EKATARENA
For a moment neither one of them speaks

ANNA
your brother
               my son

EKATARENA
Anna starts to giggle,
startling all of us

ANNA
and yes   ohh yes
I know about living the wild life

EKATARENA
oh hurray
wonderful
she stands
a performance
and all of us
become her audience
you're going to enjoy this

> ANNA
> "We're hawks and harlots here,
> In The Runaway Dog   our bistro

> CHORUS
> The walls bright with birds and flowers
> That languish in a painted cloud"

> ANNA
> "And me dressed tight in a narrow skirt

> EKATARENA
> To make sure she looks trim and slender."

ANNA
Gumilev was one of our poets

EKATARENA.
bride and groom   honeymoon in Paris
conceived a son   Lev

ANNA
and oh   the music   the paintings

> CHORUS
> "The sight of a swallow swooping free
> Sent her flying every morning."

ANNA
Modigliani   enraptured
drew sixteen portraits of naked me

EKATARENA
she's got one hanging on her bedroom wall

ANNA
when we came home again
reciting my new poems
all over St Peters . . .

EKATARENA
Leningrad

ANNA
all over Leningrad
                  "His gentle eyes so captivating
                  No way will I forget them"

OLGA
oh yes oh my
got to have that don't we
his gentle eyes

EKATARENA
two books
two of them
people reading them

ANNA
asking for my autograph

OLGA
aww   not just one but two   how nice
and what does a book taste like . . .
how does a book mend a broken neck . . .
how does a book keep you safe

when   if you read it
you wind up behind that wall

CHORUS
"Even the birds don't sing today
 And the aspen trees no longer tremble"

ANNA
Why your brother?

OLGA
I told you   I don't know

ANNA
I don't believe you

OLGA
I told you

ANNA
you didn't bother to ask

OLGA
a knock on the door

ANNA
and never a word

OLGA
oh, there were words
loud and violent

ANNA
well of course
for Comrade Mustache
our glorious leader
          words are . . .

OLGA
wait a minute
I'm sudden realizing
I know who you are
heard people talking about you
a poet   yes?   on the steps of the library?

EKATARENA ·
NKVD catches her there
beats her   kicks her
to emphasize the fact that
tbe Central Committee had issued an order
told her she must never publish her poems

ANNA
. . . his words   are weapons—
poison   swindler   whore
lying agent of the pernicious past
that's what they called me
all rolled into one

OLGA
and did you?   publish?

EKATARENA
it was like they had
closed down her life

ANNA
Mustache and Hitler
think of them, ugly face to ugly face
sitting at the table
like reflections in the mirror

EKATARENA
why are tyrants so obsessed with their hair

OLGA
did you?

ANNA
they murdered Gumilev
shot him in the street

EKATARENA
accused him of conspiracy
spent an afternoon
with a British scientist
talking British scientist stuff
said the British scientist
was a spy

ANNA
and my friend   Osip Mandelstam

CHORUS
"A night is coming that knows no dawn"

OLGA
he died

didn't he

starved and cold

in a gulag

EKATARENA
like all of us
we count our losses
find our way to another day

CHORUS
"Hand in hand we are the same."

ANNA
because he read his poem to us at a party
all about Mustache
how we laughed at what Osip wrote

EKATARENA
thin-necked chieftains all around him

ANNA
laughing eyes of a cockroach

EKATARENA
fingers fat   like worms are fat

ANNA
how we cried when we heard his angry words—
                    they never hear our pain

OLGA
and since then   no writing?

EKATARENA
job in the library

ANNA
shelving books   translating
researching the work of Pushkin
wrote essays about him
safe to do that   *him* they love
as do I

            "A dark-skin youth he wandered
            Along alleys round the lake.

            CHORUS joins her
            A century later still we hear
            The rustling echo of his footsteps."

ANNA
they crush every shred of human dignity

I tore out a thread of hair one day
put it in the book I was reading
have to laugh
like bullies in the playgound
when I came home
the hair was gone.

but

Mustache changed his mind
I have no idea why   on a whim perhaps
as I said   childish
he sudden said I could publish again
read my poems in public again

EKATARENA
oh hurray
wonderful
she stands
a performance

and all of us
become her audience

> ANNA
> "Everything is plundered, broken,
> Death flickers its wide black wings,
> The hungry yearn for a crust of bread."
>
> CHORUS
> "How do we wipe away our tears?"

EKATARENA
and here's her answer

ANNA

"In the light of day the cherry trees
Shower the city with swirling blossoms,
At night a host of constellations
Shine in the dark of the sky."

EKATARENA

a thousand people on their feet
                hey come on everybody
     applaud   cheer   loud

ANNA

but
he doesn't like it when a crowd
applauds anyone but him

EKATARENA

he had Lev arrested

ANNA

if I write another word

EKATARENA

Lev will pay the price

ANNA

my son
please
tell me your name

OLGA

Olga

EKATARENA

oh now   she's trusted you
told you things it's dangerous for her to say
return the favor
tell her things it's dangerous for *you* to say

OLGA
Nataliya

EKATARENA
beautiful

ANNA
Mustache will one day pass
but the Iliad
  Nataliya
psalms in the Bible
Sappho on her island

EKATARENA
the power of poetry

ANNA
I couldn't let him consume me
and not writing is like not breathing
I began to write

NATALIYA
oh you did it! you published!

EKATARENA
not exactly

ANNA
I put the words on paper
but then   I burned them
ten pages
fastened in my memory

EKATARENA
and what she wrote:

ANNA
"I found out how faces grow hard"

CHORUS
"How fear hides under our eyelids."

ANNA
you were carrying something to the window

EKATARENA
Anna picks up the coat
that Nataliya threw away
gives it to her

ANNA
stay

EKATARENA
She extends her hand.

ANNA
stand among us
your brother will be lonely
without you on the line

EKATARENA
smiling   Nataliya takes hold of Anna's hand
and Anna leads her to the wall.

> ANNA solo
> "How suffering is painted on our cheeks"
>
> add CHORUS
> "Like cuneiform writing on ancient tablets."
>
> add CHORUS
> "How vibrant hair turns sudden silver."
> "How a smile fades on hopeful lips."
>
> NATALIYA solo
> "How fear shivers into frigid laughter."

EVERYONE
"I pray not only for myself
"But for everyone who's standing here."

EKATARENA solo
"In the biting cold, in the summer heat"
"Beside the red deaf wall."

SMASHING

And then he repeated it
like an old man lying on the floor
instead of his bed. Where am I?

— Louise Glück

I arrive for a one-week visit
find Dad battered-down
cardigan torn and splattered
cuts on his forehead and nose

on his way to pay his gas bill
running to catch the bus
he slipped   fell   blacked out
taken by ambulance to the hospital

"they looked me over
not to worry
found nothing wrong
doing fine"

he reaches out to hold
my hand   soft and possessive

"and how are you

on holiday
are you

fancy that
coming to see me"

remembering London in 1940

six years old   I was swept up by the crowd
King's Street shops shut down quick

shoppers and shopkeepers scurried
somber silence   wrought-iron fence

Messerschmitt nose buried in the park
metallic dragon tail erect in the air

everyone swaying   old granny weeping
I ferreted my way through shuffles of feet

53

                              cockpit empty   panic   where's the pilot
                              from nowhere a tap on my shoulder

                                           Dad ruffled my hair
                                    took my hand to walk me home

later   in at the front door after a shopping spree
I'm loaded down with groceries and laundry
he waves a dish towel in my face

    "I'm sorry

    you've got to go
    you can't stay here

    Tony's coming
    he needs the room"

he turns abruptly into the kitchen
I'm Tony   how do I respond
padlock my tongue   move on
go back to the car

return with a walking stick
I've bought for him
this time he's all smiles

    "who was that bloke

    do you know him

    wanted your room
    but I told him
    get lost

    you come first"

I offer the walking stick

"oh thank you
isn't it smashing

but no
I don't need it

doing fine"

burnished metal folding like a tent pole
adjustable elastic inside   I fit it
so his hand sits tight in the handle

    "smashing! but no   really
    what will people say
    see me walking with a stick"

I show him the rubber foot
protection against a slip'n'fall

    "smashing   it truly is"
and he disappears

        he was always so active and sporty

        when my mother flew to the States
           to be with her Yankee shag

        every evening after dinner
    the two of us   left behind   bonded

        racing up and down the street
    passing and catching my rugby ball

        he ran away when he was 17
    to join the Queen's Own Hussars

        six years on the back of a horse
scrum half on the Rochdale rugby team

                              someone like that would never feel
                              he'd one day need a walking stick

I find him in the front room
stashing it behind the curtains

    "those miserable sods
    they'll try and steal it

    I know they will
    I'll kill them

    f'ever I catch them"

Barry introduces himself
a psychiatric social worker
dispatched by the hospital

he sits leaning forward facing Dad
asking his questions

    "I hope I know the answers"

do you know how old you are

    "well   of course"

how old are you?

    "I'm 89

    next May
    going to be 90

    fancy that
    90 years old"

can you tell me what day it is today

"I forget"

it's Monday afternoon

    "right   Monday
    Monday afternoon"

and is that your garden

    "yes   my garden
    can't see it proper
    these dirty windows

    just as well
    not what it used to be
    such a lovely display"

what it used to be

picturing our younger son
toddling down the red brick path

to load up with what-he-called bopples
for teatime applepie and custard

Dad and Marjorie working together
their playground on sunny afternoons

nasturtiums   lobelia   zinnias   roses
overflowering the clean-cut lawn

she frail and cautious   he bustling
sweethearts calling out to one another

do you remember being in hospital

    "when"

you fell while running for a bus

"a bus

and   and you say
I fell

oh my"

do you know you may be entitled
to a disability allowance

"do I really"

oh yes   senior citizen   living alone
the Lewisham council might think
you're eligible   can I get it for you

"well   if you say so"

no   not if I say so
it has to be because you say so

"well then
I say so"

and one by one Barry Social Worker
offers to get him—
   a hot meal delivered every Sunday
   laundry pickup and return every week
   a special phone for the hearing impaired
   with flashing lights and a raucous bell

afterwards in the front garden
Barry wonders about Dad's congestion
I tell him it was new this morning
fine yesterday but after he got up
lots of coughing   his chest hurting

Barry's response to that is simple
                          he ought to see a doctor

my response to that is wild—on Friday
        back to New York   before I go need
                to make sure he's safe   don't know
    how things work in   London   born
            in England but so what   a stranger
it's all a muddle   ask Dad about his doctor
    he can't remember   phone number
name   paperwork   my 90-year-old
                        father losing his
        mind in front of my eyes
asked neighbor Joan who lost her husband Bert
  weeks after Dad lost Marjorie
Joan who often takes care of Dad   always neighborly
        things like laundry
and spare keys   nothing about a doctor   Dad
  shaves   we go looking   the street where he thinks
the doctor has a surgery
  with his memory guess what   fuming how he
doesn't need a doctor
    not to worry   doing fine   when he's not
Barry touches my shoulder
tells me not to worry
and we chuckle
a welcome sliver of laughter
promises to ask around
and find us a doctor

next morning Dad moaning in the kitchen
on his knees surrounded by pots and pans
pulled from a cupboard under the stove

    "they've pinched
    my flipping teeth
    what do they want
    with my teeth
    I'll kill them
    f'ever I catch them"

I gently suggest perhaps
he left them on his night table
before he went to bed

    "oh I never
    I always hide them
    in this saucepan"

he hurls it thumping across the floor

even so I tell him maybe look upstairs

    "all right all right
    but it'll do no good
    they've been pinched"

he struggles to his feet leaves returns
eyes glooming down at the pots and pans
hands hanging loose teeth in his mouth

    "funny that
    every morning
    come down
    fill the kettle for tea
    scrub them clean
    my teeth

    oh well
    nowadays
    things disappear"

not just nowadays

like coming home from school
to an empty house no furniture

a week later my mother disappeared too
selling our beds helped her buy a plane ticket

into the arms of her Yankee prince charming
all the dust-ups and shout-downs at home

my school work nosediving   bottom of the class
about to be relegated from A stream to B

only person offering relief   the headmaster
I asked him to set me back a year

a thread however frail to weave a path
through the turmoils all around me

by the time the doctor arrives
Dad is stretched on the floor
seeking relief   lying on his back
clutching at knife-like jabs
the doctor kneels beside him
probes his chest   listens
presses hard on the ribs

    "why don't you
    just shoot me
    and get it over with"

he explains what's been happening—
  you have an infection
  ribs were bruised in the fall
  it hurts you to cough   to avoid
  aggravating pain in the ribs
  you suppress your cough
  which in turn generates
  fluid in the lungs

he pulls out a pad
scribbles two prescriptions
a cough suppressant
an anti-biotic
to be taken for ten days twice a day

ouch   I tell him in a whisper
about the pots and pans
no way will Dad take the pills
as required   if he takes them at all
the doctor nods   suggests
a visiting nurse can come by
every morning   every evening
would we like that

I don't hesitate   yes
we would very much like that

as he opens the door to leave
I ask if Dad's problem is dementia
he shakes his head   uncertain
looks like it
but maybe it's old age memory loss
if he knows he's forgetting things
it's hard to call it dementia

> "you two
> talking about me
>
> you should know
> I don't take fondly
> to secrets"

I squirm out of this one
just thanking Doctor for all his help

quick I head to the chemist
next door to Dad's favored bakery
get him his new medicines
back home just as quick
give him one of each   soon
he begins to feel better

> "it's a good thing
> you were here

me lying
on the floor like that
·don't know what
I would've done
on my own"

later   I find him under the table
hunting for the pills he spilled
can't restrain myself   I yell at him
hoping he hasn't taken any

"of course

it's why
we bought them
isn't it"

do you ever think of moving
into an assisted living home
the question I ask
every time I come to visit
Auntie Doris did it and she's ecstatic
everything you might need provided

every time the same answer

"well   I suppose

oh but such a bother
all this furniture

Marjorie loved it
all her decorations
she was so happy
living here"

so happy living with Dad

he blushed embarrassed when Marjorie
told me her story   with teasing-him delight

the day when Dad didn't show up for work
she and a friend dropped by to find out why

found him stretched on the floor
with a shattered gall bladder   the friend

ran to a phone box to call for an ambulance
while Marjorie found a blanket and pillow

Marjorie who watched over him in his recovery
who fed him   nursed him   held him

who was a refugee from a fist-flying husband
fragile souls joining hands in a lonely world

"I think I see her
sometimes
beside me
looking out for me"

preparing to fly home I write notes
in big black capital letters
and post them

on the telephone:
CALL BARRY SOCIAL WORKER
IF YOU NEED HELP

on the dining room table:
EVERY SUNDAY SOMEONE WILL COME
WITH A NICE HOT MEAL—EAT IT
IT'S ALL PAID FOR

on the medicine box:
DO NOT TOUCH AT ANY TIME
WAIT FOR NURSE TO COME
YOU <u>MUST</u> LET HER IN

on the front door:
WHERE'S WALKING STICK

lunchtime in New York
getting dark in London   Joan calls
says Dad knocked on her door
asked her to call the police
he imagined a strange man in his house
who cut down the roses in his garden
wrote things all over the walls
cooked a couple of sausages
getting ready to shoot him

nurse arrives   time for his pills
instead   angry   on the phone
she intends to call for an ambulance
he's out on the street dodging traffic
howling for rescue from intruders

                I'm lost   how do I respond

she gets testy   don't you realize
he's a danger to himself

                  all right   all right

two hours later Joan calls again
he's been taken to Hither Green hospital

next day   strung out from not sleeping
I call Barry Social Worker to catch up
says he's found a ward in the hospital
for elderly patients like Dad
they've sedated him to calm his agitation
put him on haloperidol   an anti-psychotic drug
keeping him in the ward for observation

I ask if I should come
he doesn't think so   not yet anyway

65

I call the number he gives me
but the nurse in the ward
tells me Dad is resting quietly
                  let's not disturb him

I call Joan to thank her for all she's been doing
she sounds tired and troubled
a notice from the gas company
waiting for payment of two old bills
threatening to cut off his gas
and   mail from the borough council
he hasn't paid his taxes in more than a year
the letter says they're taking him to court

Barry on the phone
tells me Dad will be held
in the hospital for several weeks
as for the taxes   he got a postponement
but the taxes and the bills must be paid
perhaps I should consider
taking control of Dad's financial affairs

so how do I   sitting in New York
find a lawyer in London
the answer as always   Barry Social Worker

right she says what can we do for you
she's a specialist in settling estates
first and immediate
settle with the gas company
and the borough of Lewisham
after that the court of protection
asking to be appointed receiver
giving me administrative control

the court of protection won't consider
our petition if his house is not insured
so make sure it is

all the papers I have to produce
   a copy of his will
   evidence that Dad holds outright ownership
   the patient's history
   a statement of my personal intentions
   a doctor's certification that Dad
   is not able to care for himself

his not-so history

                        front page of the Cleveland Press
            maybe turning brown in some secret drawer

            in an interview my mother told the reporter
                        Dad was captain of a battleship

                        torpedoed in the Indian Ocean
                        dead and smothered in medals

            another lie   she told the paper I was 13
                        a year less than what my passport said

            not a word about her divorce   never knew
            I had a new father until he shook my hand

Barry Social Worker tells me
a Doctor Philpot has signed
the court of protection papers
and the ward's staff has discussed
Dad's future   unanimous appraisal
he belongs in residential care

the nightmare grinds on
I contact an office called Home Finders
it takes them two weeks to get back to me
calling to say they have two recommendations
I ask them to contact the two homes
and put a hold on what's available

I call Dad as often as I can
always the same little serenade

    "they keep me here
    I'd like to go to the shops
    get a banana   a kidney pie

    still   not to worry
    they tell me
    I'll be out of here soon

    going home"

I don't have the heart
to tell him the truth

my wife Marna with me
we arrive late on a Saturday
drive to Dad's home
next morning head for the hospital
spot Dad at the end of the ward
run towards him yelling
he struggles to run towards me
fighting back his tears
a never-let-go hug

                    history repeats itself

           in the U.S Army   stationed in Frankfurt
        living with Marna in a one-room apartment

            ten years of separation from Dad
            letters at first then they stopped

          after a stormy ferry ride from France
       at a London railway station   my suitcase

     and his umbrella slammed across the platform
       as we locked our arms around each other

he turns to Marna
she also gets a hug

I hand him his walking stick

    "oh isn't this
    a beauty
    is this for me"

I nod   holding back my own tears

    "smashing
    I can use this
    having a bit of trouble
    wobble now and then
    this will come in handy"

he's lost weight   eyes bulging
razor gashes on his chin

he leads us to his bedside
at his insistence
Marna sits
on a comfy chair
while he sits on the bed

    "how are you
    are you here on holiday
    they say
    I'll be out of here soon
    not to worry
    doing fine
    going home
    where are you staying"

we tell him we slept the night
in his house   and he beams

"did you really
how did you get in
and   and how are you
 (fancy that
here on holiday
and coming to see me
smashing
this walking stick
going to come in handy
where are you staying"

throw ourselves into the whirlwind
dismantling my father's existence

        room by room   inventory and cleanup
every cupboard
            drawer   scrap of paper photo
envelope booklet brochure   what's to be thrown
                        away   what's to be sold
            Marjorie's crusted cosmetics
    removed from the medicine cupboard   make
an appointment with
                lawyer   call a handyman
    for when   what needs throwing away   gets
                    stashed in garbage bags
    lawyer   fingering
            papers piled infront of her   his
will   national savings
                        bonds   pension papers   deed
for the house   appointment
            with bank to create an account in my name
                to pay for his upcoming medical
and housing   I sit for a moment and cry
        not because I'm sad
                        which I am but because
            I feel so helpless
        lawyer gives us names of estate agents   make
            appointments with two of them   both

tut-tut   repairs needed   affects the price   each
makes the same offer we choose
                 the more congenial   ask
      him for a name
of someone who can buy the furniture
                  take it away
   lots of knickknack treasures gathered in front
room   invite Joan to come browse
       take anything that pleases   enchanted
        by a trifle set
   crystal bowl
  with serving bowlets oh could she   her son
and family coming to visit and this
  would make Christmas dinner so meaningful

she joins us with a box
for the trifle set
kicks us out of the kitchen
so she can boil us a cuppa
when it's poured
and we're sitting together
ask her to choose a vase
for the gratitude roses
we've bought her

                          remembering another bouquet

                       the posy of purple violets
          Dad gave me as he put me on the plane

         told me my mother was crazy about violets
          but when we arrived in Newfoundland

                 a fuel and breakfast stopover
given a guide on Laguardia arrival procedures

          transporting plants severely forbidden
     unsure in a foreign country inexperienced

          imagining punishments in store for me
    upset most about breaking my promise to Dad

           off the plane headed for the coffee shop
            I stuffed the violets in my pocket

       runway snow bulldozed into a massive wall
          I stopped to dig a tunnel for them

       plastered a fluffy snowball on top of them
     in the darkness of dawn   not a word to anyone

time to visit the nursing homes
the first on the coast east of London
on a gentle slope overlooking the water
monumental toffee-nose building
in the middle of a meadow of marigolds
the director in a tailored suit meets us
in the waiting room leads us through a maze
endless corridors staircases corners four rooms
each available for a different price
dining room at the end of another corridor
dozens of tables dressed in pink
down another set of stairs to a game room
with a snooker table Dad would like that

four spacious lounges each with a TV
each tuned to one different no-choice channel
many of the patients in the largest
mostly grey-haired women lost among
the cushions staring at nothing

very elegant but Dad would wander
lost morning noon and night

home number two located south of London
close to Gatwick Airport
a building at the end of a cul-de-sac

Ruth Molloy   the deputy matron
lying in wait for us
a hefty lass   a warm-hearted smile
a broad Lancashire accent   glows
when we tell her Dad be from Rochdale

takes us on a tour of the building
downstairs a big pool   heated water
cherry picker for dunking wheelchair patients
nearby a hairdresser   laundry   game room
then she shows us the new quarters
ready to be launched as a special ward
a program geared to dementia therapy
private rooms for a dozen patients
a local doctor visiting every afternoon

we head back to Hither Green
tell Barry Social Worker
we're going with number two
Barry disappears into the nurse's station
emerges a litttle later to tell us
within a week or two a nurse
someone Dad trusts will drive him down

and could we have available for transport
the furniture and clothes he might need

time to talk with Dad
several comfy chairs in a hallway
Barry brings us a round of tea
starts the conversation

do you remember me?

    "vaguely"

Barry Purnell   your social worker

    "oh   yes   Barry"

do you know where we are?

    "hospital"

do you know why

    "not really

    been having
    difficulties

    but doing fine
    get around
    my walking stick
    my best friend"

how long have you been here

    no answer

well   actually you've been here since August

    "have I really
    well I'm dashed"

and do you know what day it is today

    "I for get"

Thursday

    "that's right
    Thursday"

do you know what month it is

    "you tell me"

November

"November
is that true
November"

I nod him yes

"well I'm dashed
and you say
I've been here
since August"

he works it out on his fingers

"oh dear"

he sits stricken

a moment when I sat stricken

the lights in the carriage flickered off
the train pulled to a stop in the dark

I moved curious to the window
but Dad reached out   pulled me back

a train on the neighbor track thundered by
not a squidgeon of light inside

I could hear our engine wheezing
but never a hint of moving   I asked

what was going on   Dad shushed me again
told me to sit back close my eyes and sleep

thought we were on our way to Rochdale
to visit his sister Polly and her husband

                                       Uncle Tom   a jolly old trickster
         always tugging at my ear to find me a penny

                  somewhere nearby sudden explosions
        Dad was wordless   flung his arm around me

I pull close to him to talk softly
Dad the thing is even if you've been here
all this time   they aren't doing all that much
to help you you need more than they can provide

    "well yes
    you always want
    to get better
    don't you"

you need some special help

    "I don't know

    well
    if you say so"

I've found a home in Horsham   all sorts of special ways
of taking care of someone with problems like yours

    "Horsham

    I don't know

    where is that"

near Crawley   Gatwick

    "so you're saying
    I need
    special help

well now
what kind
of special help
if I might ask
would that be

like this
a hospital

a room of your own   with a door

"ah   a room

of my own

and a window"

yes Dad   a window   you can see outside
trees   flowers   lots of birds   sunlight

"well   I suppose
I should

I'd like that
a window

and birds

but look
may I think
about this"

of course

"you see

doing fine
they tell me
soon I'm going

going home
to my house
and the shops

so why
would I need
to go to   to..."

Horsham

"why should I
be going there
when soon

I'm going home

aren't I

going home"

I reach out to take his hand

when Dad was no longer dead

with the promise of marriage in the air
I broke my silence   told Marna

Dad was alive   somewhere unknown
her response   she wanted to meet him

papers from a legal office in London
asking me to waive my inheritance

total mystery   address confidential
so Marna asked her friend Bobbie

planning a trip with her college choir
singing in cathedrals all over Europe

                              to look in the London phone book
                              find men with my father's name

                         better than that   she knocked on doors
                              came home with a fuzzy photo

Dad fumes   some miserable sod has hung
a jacket in his wardrobe   insists it's not his
he lights a cigarette
    I ask him
if he'd like to take it outside
jumps at the chance   puts the jacket on
grabs his best friend
we stroll the street   find a bench
listen to the birds in concert mode

he fidgets   something on his mind
lights another cigarette
grumbles at me   begging me
to fetch the car   take him home

I don't have the heart
to yet again tell him
I've sold his house

I steer him back to the nursing home
at the door trembling he refuses to go in
I push buttons and the door opens

he's amazed   laughs   how did I do it
I make up some numbers   6 7 8 5
storing it away 6587 chuckling
on his way to his window
        being cared for   safe

)

About the Author

Tony Howarth, editor for dramatic writing with *The Westchester Review*, is a playwright, director, former journalist, retired in 1991 after twenty-eight years as a high school and college teacher of English and theatre. William Wordsworth helped him survive adolescence, inspired him to write poetry of his own, but as as a college freshman he found *a sense sublime of something far more deeply interfused* did not fit well in a climate devoted to the work of Eliot and Pope. He adjusted his ambitions to journalism, in Cleveland; Meriden, Connecticut; the US Army; Lancaster, Pennsylvania; Indianapolis; and New York City, where he was editor of the editorial page of *The World-Telegram and Sun*. Disillusioned after a printers' strike and the assasination of John F. Kennedy, he turned to teaching, where he was asked to develop a theatre program, which in turn led to a list of professional credits, including a dozen plays and a musical presented off-Broadway; full lengths include *Thornwood*, which won a Drama League grant, produced at Circle Rep and the Mint Theatre in New York City, colleges across the U.S., Amsterdam, Tanzania, made into an award-winning indie film, *Slings and Arrows*. For many summers he directed musicals at the College Light Opera Company in Falmouth, Massachusetts. He began writing poetry again in 2009 after a visit to Wordworth's Dove Cottage (clouds and daffodils) in England's Lake District. His poetry, developed at the Hudson Valley Writing Center under the treasured guidance of Jennifer Franklin and Fred Marchant, has appeared in many magazines, among them *Chronogram*, *The Naugatuck River Review*, a magazine in England *Obsessed with Pipework*, *The Connecticut River Review*, *Raven's Perch*, *The Sow's Ear*, the Grayson Press anthology *Forgotten Women*. And a play published by The Westchester Review called *The Wedding Ring*, a moment in the life of who else but William Wordsworth. *Wild Man of the Mountain*, his first drama in verse, was published by Broadstone Books in 2021.